Prologue:

My Fathers Are With Me

I have lived with water and felt wrong without it. My family has been in and on and near Minnesota water for five generations and no matter where we move we come back to it. Earliest in my ambulatory life was walking the beach and picking up shells and running my fingers through wet sand and water water in my eyes in front of my eyes and my family around me. It moves and it moves me in flow and depth and ripple. It has moods and power and never stops. It is eternal and will remain always changing after I am gone. I do my best prayer time on the lake or river or on shore looking and listening. I even like ice-time because it intimates of the water beneath and the revelation of spring. The plains are deadly, Black Hills grotesque. The ocean is marvelously foamy but dank with history. The mountains are stirring but claustrophobic, always poking at the eye and so I need the Mississippi in its youth and agelessness and beginning. Water flows like the blood of the continent, sustaining the land and the trees and me. This is the Mississippi and its lakes and my home.

The infant Mississippi flows north, then east, then southeast, forming a barbless hook of young river clinging to northern Minnesota, softening occasionally into lakes where it gains strength and resolve before it reaches its purposeful maturity of riverboats and barges and commerce flowing south to a jazz-rich delta before expiring in the sea. For the last century my family has called that hook of waters home.

My great grandfather came to Cass Lake in 1901 to minister to the good Lutheran loggers and, in the tradition of his father, to convert the Chippewa. He also had a useful skill—he was a physician. There is a family legend that one day in the pulpit early in his ministerial career, before he moved to Cass Lake, he began hemorrhaging from the throat while preaching. He and his congregation thought he was dying. He was so surprised when he didn't die that he went to medical school to find out why not and got his M.D. in the process. Whether the legend is true or not, when he arrived in Cass Lake he had two vocations: medicine and the church. He set up a medical office while founding a church—Trinity Lutheran Church. The church is still there; the medical office is long gone.

He came from a long line of Lutheran clergymen. In Norway, the ministers were the public school teachers because there were no public schools. My mother's grandmother, born in Norway, used to talk of "reading for the minister," meaning learning how to read from the minister. In Cass Lake he did not perform that function; it had public schools, so literacy was no longer the minister's business, except for Scriptural reading. His descendants moved in that direction—teaching— and not in the other longer tradition of religion. I have a notion that tradition faded due to long contact with Minnesota wilderness and American Indians.

My great great grandfather, the first Christensen in America, came from Norway to preach the gospel, moving quickly to what was then the very rough country of the mid-Western border states. He spent his career moving from one settlement and Indian village to another, ever hopeful of saving new souls. Eventually he found his way back toward the center of the continent and finally died in North Dakota. That tradition of ministering to settlers and trying to minister to Indians

4

is the history his son, my great grandfather Gustav Albert, brought to Cass Lake and the Chippewa. Cass Lake, like other small Minnesota towns around it, was settled late, mostly by people coming back east from the Dakotas where they had failed as farmers. The area was settled as a kind of backwash—people had gone through on the way to the farmland of Dakota and remembered it as a natural paradise, magical after the endless winds and woodless winters of the plains. When he arrived, Cass Lake was a little lumber town as raw as anything we ever saw in a Western movie, and the Chippew—now Ojibwe to Christensens and other polite people, but Chippewa then—were living pretty traditional lives.

In the newspaper accounts of the time he is often mentioned doing civic things—judging floats in the Fourth of July parade, acting as Captain Cass in the Founders Day water carnival, but always referred to as Dr. Christensen, not Reverend. Nowhere in those pieces is his ministry mentioned. It's as though he is greatly respected as a doctor, but his religious contributions don't make the paper.

In a way G.A. "Doc" Christensen was a great success with the Chippewa. Few of them converted and attended church services, but they brought their babies and old people to his office and he treated them with care and affection. He rode a lot of miles in his one horse buggy in all weather to aid in birthing and healing and dying. He was respected—even loved—in that time before the Depression and World War II and boarding schools and church sponsored forced relocation/reeducation of Chippewa babies. There were few racial conflicts within the church itself in those days because Indians mostly didn't attend, and, according to my surviving relatives, probably wouldn't have been very welcome by the white parishioners anyway, though the Christensens would have been pleased to see them.

The ministerial tradition was broken when G.A.'s son, Norman, came home from World War I. God got lost somewhere on the Marne and the line of Christensen missionaries was broken. There would be no medical school and no seminary and no theology for Norm Christensen. He founded the Cass Lake American Legion in the name of his buddy, Jack Kimball, who died next to him on a field near Chateau Thierry, and started a drug store. His spirits were bottled and so was the healing he offered. He earned good words from the community and the tribe because he carried so many people on credit or took things like venison or wild rice or vegetables in payment. He was kind with what he could be. He could not be a minister. He supplied nostrums and left the homilies to others.

I don't know what G.A. thought or felt when he realized the generations of ministerial devotion had been broken, but he had great hopes for my father, the first grandson, as a minister in the making. He died when Dad was a teenager, so he didn't have the chance to see what Dad became, or to directly influence his choices. It was, however, because of G.A.'s choice in 1901 that Dad, born in 1921, was the first Christensen raised in daily contact with the Chippewa. His babysitters were Indian women; his schoolmates were Indian children. He and his younger brother Paige wrestled with Indians, went fishing with Indians, hunted with Indians. Their grandfather's patients were largely Chippewa; their father's drugstore customers were largely Chippewa.

Daily life for Dad and Paige was as much contact with Indians as it was with Scandinavians.

Norm and his wife Helen raised Dad and Paige in the church with regular and mandatory attendance and confirmation. Dad played the piano and organ for the Lutheran weddings and funerals—the old people in Cass Lake remember him for that—and even thought about becoming a minister in addition to becoming an English professor, a job he settled on at the age of three. He carried with him a kind of earth/lake/sky spirituality that made him, as a young man, as at home in the woods as he was in the church, which might have set him up for the trouble that was coming.

In 1939 Norm and Helen sent Dad to St. Olaf, the boarding school for good Scandinavian Lutherans, where Dad learned Lutheran discipline—the discipline of daily chapel, required religion classes, and doctrine not to be questioned. It wasn't nearly as malignant as the boarding schools the Chippewa were sent to, but St. Olaf killed the minister in the making he brought to the campus and very nearly ended his academic career too. Dad was not one who appreciated demands for mindless obedience—the strictures of Lutheranism as it lived at St. Olaf led him to leave the church. In fact, one day he left St. Olaf when he was supposed to be in chapel and hitchhiked to Florida, sleeping in ditches along the way. In 1940 students didn't leave campus without permission. When he came back broke, tired, and hungry the president let him back into school after a blistering scolding, in the tradition of church sponsored school discipline, and Dad, properly chastised, finished his degree without further rebellion. He went on for a master's and a doctorate, but not in private religious schools. He'd had enough of them.

So he became a professor without religion—formal religion—but he was often treated as though he were a minister by people who didn't know him. People he met on the streets or in stores would tell him things about themselves that aren't normally shared with strangers. His students told him intimacies he didn't seek. Colleagues came to him for spiritual advice. Somehow he appeared trustworthy without trying to, and so he carried the troubles of many. During his adult life he seldom spoke of either Lutherans or Indians; he associated with both, but left matters of religion to the religious and race to the racists.

His way of worship was water. He sat on a lake with a fishing pole and contemplated. He developed or maintained a spirituality far more like that nature consciousness whites associate with Indians than that of his Lutheran forebears. He watched trees and noticed a little hill that he wrote about fifty years later and studied a creek (he said "crick") and read papers written by white and Ojibwe students. That is the church he taught me. G.A.'s decision to bring his mission to Cass Lake meant his grandson became a vaguely Indianized ex-Lutheran, and ended the Christensen tradition of ministry forever.

In my childhood there was no church. I was raised—the first non-Lutheran generation since the 17th Century—to choose for myself. Paige's family maintained the tradition, but my parents encouraged me to attend any church I chose any time I wanted, so I did. I went to the churches my childhood friends attended and my parents made no comment. In my adult life, as I came to know the Christensen family history, I gradually realized that I had to deal with two issues regarding that history—one of them being religion, the other one masculine identity.

My religious instruction from my father was to take me fishing. He showed me how to rig tackle, use a net, and test for depth before there were electronic boxes that did that. Better though, he taught me to be quiet in the boat—spirits need quiet—and to watch weather. I recall sitting just outside the reedbed fifty yards from shore—land that his grandfather bought and his father sold, just across the outlet of the Mississippi from Indian land we weren't allowed on—and he taught me to watch the sky. Anyone in doubt about spiritual life need only watch the sky, and even better, the sky in the water. There is power behind the sky and beneath the water, magic beyond the ken of humans.

Sun and waves have magic. If you sit in a boat on a windy day you can look in one direction toward the reflected sun and see a glitter on the waves strong enough to make your eyes ache and look the other direction with the sun and see water as dark as ink. Brightness and darkness simultaneously, each in the other, opposites.

The each in each other opposites of sky and water were the peace in our lives, the flow we returned to for connection and restoring faith in the eternity of things. In winter that flow was hidden beneath sheets of ice far too thick to see through, but we kept faith in ice time that water beyond our vision still moved, and with breakup we would see the river flow north again.

The spirituality my father taught me feels nothing like the hubris I associate with the idea of missionary attempts to convert the Chippewa to Christianity. One has to be far more sure of one's rightness than I am to feel that the Chippewa need, for their own sakes, to

9

convert to, and submit to, the disciplines of Lutheranism. In my thirties I developed a queasiness in my thinking about my Minnesota roots. I found that when I thought about the Christensen relationships with the Chippewa, I was pleased with G.A.'s medical contributions and Norm's drug store service and Dad's offerings of literacy, but I was embarrassed by G.A.'s religious efforts. I knew them to be well intentioned, but I associated them with the horrors of the boarding schools and forced assimilation that Christians imposed on the Indians, and I had difficulty reconciling good intentions with such grief.

During my uncle Paige's last days, I learned of more family history regarding the church and race. One bitterly cold winter two or three decades ago, the tensions about welcoming Indians in the very church G.A. founded came into the open when the pastor let some homeless Indians sleep in the heated basement of the church. Some parishioners were horrified at the thought of Indians sleeping in the basement, making comments about such things as the safety of the communion wine. After considerable conflict within the still mostly white congregation, the pastor and part of the congregation, including Paige and his wife, Lucille, left Trinity Lutheran to form a new fellowship. Paige and Lucille never stopped regretting the loss of G.A.'s church to racist conflicts among Christians. Indeed, when Paige died his funeral service was held in the American Legion post his father founded, as the church his grandfather founded was no longer a welcoming place. This move is one development in the Christensen history of church and race that I can approve of, though it still leaves me with a powerful distaste for the darker side of church politics.

And where, in this talk of Christensen service and ministering and teaching and public life, are the women? I don't even know the name of G.A.'s wife, as I have heard her referred to only as "Grandma Christensen." She must have had a name, but it doesn't appear in my picture of the Christensen legend. Perhaps that is my point: the Christensen name is the defining designator in our patriarchal family. Through this century Christensen men have been supported by women who came to the name through marriage. Each of those women was or is a powerful presence, respected and loved. Each has held the Christensen family together. None has received the public recognition the men have.

So where are and have been the women? Well, they've been serving supper in the church basement, teaching the kids, running an Eastern Star chapter, tutoring disadvantaged kids, running a mental health association, volunteering for non-profit organizations, and taking care of the matters that hold the social fabric together—the fabric that supports people like ministers and doctors and professors. They have been doing these things without public recognition, and none of these women seem to care about that. Instead, they have taken pleasure in the accomplishments of the Christensen men and then quietly gone about doing the things that make society civil. As my life progressed into middle age, I came to realize that I was more interested in following the examples of the women in my life as I conduct my daily affairs, than I am in thinking about my role being defined by my work. This has provoked a broadening consciousness of the relationships among masculine identity, women, and work.

Some things about women and work are changing. Beginning with Dad's mother, Helen, and continuing

11

with his wife, Eleanor, and Paige's wife, Lucille, and carried on by my sister Ruth, my wife, Caroline, and Paige and Lucille's daughters, Karen and LuAnne (hear their names) the Christensen women have carried on public careers. Each is respected; each contributes. All have taught me, through conversation and example, how to behave in public life. The men have taught me, in some small ways, how to succeed in public life and how to live a private spiritual life. The women in my family have taught me far more about how to be a human interacting with others than have the men, and yet, traditions die hard. Residues of patriarchy remain.

When Paige died, I became the oldest male Christensen save one distant cousin—a status I have never desired. Too many men have died too young; to become the family patriarch at 42 is all too sharp a reminder that there are no male generational buffers between me and eternity. That role was brought home at Paige's funeral. Paige's wife and daughters asked me to speak at that funeral, though all three are older than I am. I can only suspect that asking me to do that was a function of my new status—the status of a reluctant patriarch.

Dad is dead now, his presence as eternal as the waters he worshipped, and so is his brother and his father and his father's father, and what I have left of those men is a non-Lutheran spirituality, a love of literacy, mixed feelings about Christensen relationships with Indians, and a tendency to turn to the water for quiet. These things, some newspaper clippings, and memories of days on the lake with Dad are finally the legacy of my great-grandfather, who came to Cass Lake, Indians, literacy, and spiritual life at the beginning of this century. I, at the end of the century, am the last remnant of that male legacy, living out my life on that same infant river, fishing the same lakes, watching the sky, being quiet in the boat, and keeping the faith in ice-time.

Keeping the faith is also my female legacy. Mom is alive and doing volunteer work, getting no recognition for it, and continuing to enjoy my success as a professor in the same department of the same university where Dad built his career. Her example, along with that of Helen and Lucille and Caroline and Ruth and Karen and LuAnne (hear their names!), is the legacy I carry as I try to support my family, do my own volunteer work, and try to be a decent man. This is my masculine identity. This is the male—and female—ethos of the surviving patriarch of a family named Christensen.

A Sense of Wool

a sense of wool

my father gave me his old wool robe—
burgundy with pale piping
around the collar and lapel
so that when the robe is tied
closed
the piping circles my neck and heart

the sleeves have been hemmed up
so they don't quite reach my wrists;
my mother shortened them
almost thirty years ago.
I'm not quite what my father was
and the sleeves remind me of that

wool holds the past

my father
wore wool shirts for outside
and wool suits for dress-up
and always that robe at home:
I smell him in that robe,
a good man/father smell
of sitting in his lap
while we read the calendar together
and then, breathing him in that robe,
I smell the man
who knew that a small boy needed to
go fishing with his father

my father had his father's
wool jacket—my mother keeps it
in the basement because it is ugly;
my father said he could smell
his father in that jacket
and when I try I smell something
that isn't wool or basement
and then my mother says she too
smells my father's father.

I wonder what my father thought
when he wore the jacket
his father wore almost fifty years ago.

wool holds the past

so when I don't fit right in the world
I put on my father's robe and
in its man smell and its
intimations of fathers and sons and its
piping around my neck and heart
the short sleeves don't matter much

for my fathers are with me
and I fit
in a sense of wool

Opener

He took time
and we opened.

He taught me—
to be quiet in the boat,
to tie knots in monofilament,
to test the water for depth,
to follow the fish when netting,
to take time.
We never missed opening.

This year time has taken him
to depths
not yet open to me,
but I test the water,
tie on new tackle
follow the fish
take time.

I am quiet in the boat.

Vision

After his burial
I walked alone,
to the end of the dock
jutting out into family waters.
High overhead, waiting,
flying in one tight circle,
were three eagles
soaring in the sun.
I sent words
with my eyes:
"Father, are you up there?"
and one eagle
broke the circle
made a single broad slow swoop
around me
and lifted toward the sky,
lifting my eyes with it,
slowly rising,
wings stroking strongly, surely
toward the sun;
the son,
my eyes running unblinking in fierce radiance,
faced the terrible beauty
leaving,

dark form diminishing,
wing action fading to tiny distant dot
until it was beyond
seeing.
Two remaining eagles
continued circling,
steadfast in their sky knowledge,
until I, the son, strode off the dock,
stepping onto shore,
seeing.

Rage

He was a raging fuckup
through all his life;
his mother said
he was born angry,
battling his blanket,
battering at her breast.

At ten or twelve—
sullen, sucking his lip,
a grunting euphoria
of too angry
too happy too angry
too sad too angry
too anything but always
too angry
to be

At 17 he discovered malt
made him more,
more of whatever was too much;
when stewed
he boiled.

At 35 he discovered treatment
and talked. And talked.
All childhood had fucked him:
Having siblings. Moving.
Changing high schools. Football knees.
Then people fucked him:
Goddamn women. Drunks.
Bosses. Bankers. Lawyers.

Then he was sober again—
furnace banked,
embers waiting beneath
the blanket of talk.

he sways,
looming,
liquor swollen nose
running
beneath bleared, bilious eyes,
face lined and scarred
with bottled rage

he slurs,
hating,
liquor swollen words
running
beneath bleared, bilious mind,
brain lined and scarred
with bottled rage

Bird

A bird died.
It was too little.

A songbird
perched on wire
high above
my brother.

I watched
my brother
shoot at the bird.
The bird sang.

My brother said
"You try."

I was too little
to be trusted
with guns.

I shot the bird.

I looked at the bird
on the ground.
Its eyes were open,
cold.
They did not forgive me.

My brother said
"Good shot."

I went into the house.
My mother's eyes were open,
cold.

I went to my room.
I hid from the eyes.
I cried for the bird.

We were too little.

forgive me, bird.
Forgive,
my brother.

Evocation

my closet is a charnel house
of dead men's clothes;
shirts and sportcoats,
parkas and sweaters

most fit easily;
my father and my brother
holding me in their sleeves

but sweaters take impressions—
shadows stretching belly, shoulder—
so the sweaters
hang like shrouds—
for sweaters take impressions—
Old Spice, English Leather—
or some more intimate essence
not my own

when I wear the sweaters
I walk in shadows
and the smell of death

My mother sits alone
at a picnic table
against a backdrop of
lake sand sky and
ghosts.

My mother and the table
shield me from
ghosts in boats
with stringers and laughter,
ghosts on the dock
with waves and nightfall.

My mother and the table
sit solidly,
braced against storms and spirits,
but they are weathering
while the ghosts
grow brighter,
beckoning from the not-here
of childhood family
and unseasoned boards.

My grandfather's grandfather
stands erect
in liturgical robes,
long Scandinavian head too large, brow too high,
dominating a face softened only
by the dark beard,
carefully trimmed,
shadowing lip and jaw and throat.

His eyes focus beyond the borders
of a century old photograph,
cupped hands bearing an open book,
long stern face eternally calm,
secure in his salvation.

Mama Watches the Fishermen

A purple place—rock and water:
sun glitter on water foam
waves wallow with wind

The waves crash
on stone pilings
and fall hissing away
under the long concrete slab
pointing sharp angled
into the lake.

My six year old,
in tennis shoes and frayed blue jeans,
shiny white little-blond-boy hair fluttering,
is dancing on the dock—
on tennis shoe toes
my boy is dancing—
slapping papa's plaid back.

I hear him over the wind—
the wind bringing him to me
over the crash and the hiss—
"I caught one I caught one let's show Mom"
And the wind and the boy and the man
come to me.

Inner Speech

At the kitchen table,
with words
my mother couldn't hear.

They sounded,
they sang in my mind,
but I wasn't speaking.

My mother couldn't hear.
I could think,
I could hear words

there at the kitchen table,
a private conversation—
myself the only listener,

myself the single orator—
as my mother folded laundry,
deaf to my silent speech.

Picnic

Norways framing
black fire grate
and splinter-rich table

kindling box
("Are you big enough to carry this?")
secure in six year old arms

striding importantly
the needle-packed
trail, stopping to watch

another family—
white-striped skunks
(What are they, Dad?"

"Be still, Son. Just watch.")—
striding importantly
the needle-packed

trail, stopping to watch
another family,
mother suspicious,

confronting, family to family,
the space between
a pine silence.

Sniffing busily,
mother blackness turns
and leads into the Norways,

surrendering the grate
and table and trail
to father and son

and kindling box
held secure by
a six year old

standing importantly.

Twin

From the mirror
a man looks at me
he isn't satisfied with what he sees
he awards no sympathy
no forgiveness
his eyes are bloodshot blue
I do not see them blink
I stare, linked eye to I,
but he is stronger—
I blink;
when I see again
he is still
looking at me

I would think
two men so alike
could see through eyes
to softer spaces
but there is only wall
behind him,
and in the mirror
there is only wall
behind me,
and glass between us

Lamp

My grandfather
lets a lamp out
of a diamond
willow
log.
My uncle
places the lamp
on a smooth
pine
stand.
My friend
fixes the
socket,
switch
and
cord.
     Three men light the night.

Grandmother's Old Love

We slept spoon fashion—
first this side,
then that.

It's forty years since he warmed my back.

Forty years ago
he was dying in my lap,
looking up as I shouted
Get the doctor!
and saying,
For me?

It's forty years
and I'm so old
—so old—
he wouldn't know me.

But still,
sometimes,
I think
If only my lover could lie here
next to me,
spoon fashion.

The bed is cold,
the nights are so long,
and still I reach for him.

Forty years.

Witness

He is solid, standing firmly,
chest held high, arms muscular;
he sobs sternly.

"I will rely on my faith;
faith is my solace."
That is his testament.

I cannot see a man sorrow
without sorrow,
but I have no faith.

No one is with me,
but I am with him.
His grief is my grief.

I am his witness;
"is"
is my testament.

I have been privy to secret grief;
I grow large
with more than merely me.

Witness the if-ness
of a searching
of souls:

When will I belong?
Must I rely forever
on dearly loved strangers?

Witness the is-ness
of a witness
of souls:

I wake up thinking
I have heard
my own epitaph

I do not remember the words.
Will my epitaph be
"He Touched but Never Embraced"?

I embrace grief;
I witness his is;
I remember my own:

I called my sister
to say our brother was dead.
She took the word quietly.

There is no peace
in knowing grief
before others.

Grief witnessed;
grief remembered.
Tomorrow grief is.

I will not be here tomorrow.
Tomorrow there is no is.
Today I witness is.

Your face
delights me
the bump
on your nose
hair that
caresses
your ear
and touches
your jaw
and frames
your throat
lips
you offer
tips
of fingers
on my brow
light
that surrounds
you
when you are
gone

pining

trees pine for sky,
reaching for unreachable spaces

they reach well;
they are good at reaching;
whether bare or leafed or needled,
they reach steadily,
season by season

but branches cannot grasp

roots grasp earth
in an encouragement
of reaching;
but branches cannot grasp stars or sky;
branches embrace air,
but air slips through
branches
    bend in their reaching,
but trees cannot give up their grasp on earth
and so branches, betrayed, must return,
while air moves on,
leaving trees
rooted and
reaching

barefoot travelers
know the earth
through beach and twig
and stone;
feet find pebbles and know
the newness of dew,
branches bend beneath the foot,
sand gives way
and regains itself
as travelers move on
in the harmony of
soles

cut

my razor edged journal
depository of my best
curses
cut me

In my back pocket
is a black plastic comb
I bought from Old Man Cross
of Cross Barber Shop
for ten cents
in 1967
I have carried it every day
for twenty-nine years.
It is curved
to the shape
of my rump
and some of the teeth
are bent
so it looks ragged as if
it would make my hair
bunch in thick strands and
thin
It doesn't work
that way
though
the hair takes the comb
as a guide
but then
falls
into arrangements
of its own choice
after the comb has
passed

The comb still does its duty
guiding hair and
hugging my butt
in a plastic
gap-toothed reminder
of 1967
when I let my hair
grow out
from close-cropped to
combable length
before my hair
developed
gaps
of its own

so many eyes
full of sound
unspoken,
opaque
like clouded
marbles

English Teacher and Sophomore Motorhead

She is
a silver-gray Ramcharger
with strong teeth
and chrome skirts

the ram's head
meeting classes
with decorative red-pencil horns—
classy Warriner's running boards
and mudflaps to keep
writing clean and rustfree.

He is
a wooden flatbed trailer
attached to her heavyduty hitch
(she came with a towing package)
with a two inch ball and flat black
wiring harness,
being pulled in
the strong 318
Dodge draft,
choking on exhaust.

Lecture

Bloodsuckers.
They think I know something,
and they want it.
They think I'm a tease,
like a stripper who knows
what's under her g-string
but wants to leave the watchers
guessing.
My questions, they think,
are like a flip of skirt
or two tossing tassels
covering the things that matter
and leading the eye and mind
—bump and grind—
astray.
Their eyes watch me
doing my dance,
while their pencils move
in time to my trickiest steps,
their mouths open
as they imagine
sucking in what I know.
They do not guess
that I do not know
what is hidden by my sequined questions
and that I am wondering
how to make my exit
—booboopadoop—
unbloodied.

Daughter Smiles

Where do they go?
The little ones
that hug and stare and ask questions
and smile sometimes.

They go to school.
They learn to ask to go to the bathroom
but never, never to ask
why teachers say such dumb things.

They learn to respond to bells
like dogs in a psychology experiment,
and to sit in neat rows
like soldiers in formation;
it's no wonder
they don't smile anymore.

You used to smile.
You'd ask me
"Why is blue?"
I'd say
"Because you opened your eyes"
and you'd giggle and hide behind the couch.

Now you go to school and you've learned.
You've taken in your lessons
and you know about bells and rules
and rows and passes
and when you come home
you slam your books on the table.
I'm afraid.
If I ask you "Why is blue?"
or something else equally silly,
will you smile?

students (in poems)

students
in dormitories
and libraries and rented rooms,
struggling to read
poems,
making dusty, foreign
work of

—students,
carrying treasured poems
clipped from newspapers
in wallets and purses,
who tape poems
to their refrigerators
and bathroom mirrors
and walls,
next to posters
and pennants
and pictures
and other
gifts of the heart,
who send Hallmark
poems
to their fathers
to say
I love you,
and secretly write
poems
but fear
other people's
poems,

afraid other people have
more words or
more heart or
more love,
but knowing
in poem—
reading Houseman,
"Teacher, this is stupid stuff"
and living
poems:
"My father died today"
(the magic)
"My boyfriend is seeing someone else"
(of love)
"There was a party on the second floor
          and I was up all night babysitting my room-
mate
    and that's why I was falling asleep in class"
(lives richly)
"She doesn't understand"
(in poems)

spring dance

a woman dances with children
like a maid in a minuet of poppets and scarves.

she smooths through schools of
child-voiced murmurs,
humming her play-along laughter.

like minnows,
children scatter
and come together
and split and come together
in a game of
someone touches someone you're it.

she skims near the walk,
then dances away spinning,
dancing and spinning,
drawing the children
around her.

she shimmers light
footed to the littlest child,
touching a gentle you're it.

he follows her graciously,
sure of his welcome and of

someone to touch.
he wraps his arms around her legs,
his face pressed firmly
between her knees,
holding his partner you're it.

she caresses the back of his suppliant head,
each hand welcoming
someone to touch,
and shivers
in her
grace.

Spectre

Tears leaking
across his face
and into his whiskers like
a windshield star-shatter,
mucus draining like rain
off the umbrella
of his mustache
and down the creases from
the corners of his nostrils
into the Biblical mass of beard,
spittle like sea foam
on the whiskers of his lower lip,
swaying tendrils of sputum
wobbling with each step,
drawn in and expelled
with each grunting breath,
each voiced exhalation
of rumbling terror;
stumbling madly, purposefully
through pedestrians scattering
like startled park pigeons,
unblinking focus on
manic dimension,
feral eyes of nightsweats,
glaring hell down
his aisle of white-lipped
silent spectators.

Taut

Butterfly comes to rest
on final eye of
my fishing
rod
my fingers
testing tension
can not know its weight

Custodial Care

He lectures,
"Study hard
or you might
grow up to be
a janitor."

I wash his blackboard,
sweep his floor,
scrub his lectern,
think of filth:

"Janitor
in a drum,
beat me,
pound my skin,
etch it with acid
strong enough to clean
shit off porcelain;
brush it, polish it,
until it reflects
your image."

Drain

Every morning before breakfast
I walked through the wards
and emptied catheter bags,
portable bladders
with plastic urethras inserted
into humans who drained
away
as they slept.
The catheter bags
had little rubber penises
clamped
by metal devices that,
loosened,
allowed the bags to empty
in streams like those of men
or dogs
urinating.
I walked from ward to ward
releasing metal clamps
and directing the flow
from rubber penises
into a plastic jar.
I knew by the smell

who would die next.
The smell
Is the yellow
of poisoned air
and the scum
of stagnant ponds
announcing the triumph
of single-celled
wriggling things
feeding.
Every morning before breakfast
I walked through the wards
smelling rubber and
yellow.
At breakfast
I ate eggs
with runny yolks.

Reflection

I see skin
stretched and released
like tired elastic
until it won't
resume its shape
any longer

When I look away
skin smooths
and lovers kiss
and tomorrow
is coming

Fisherman

muscle of forearm
battling bone,
angle of wrist
controlling tension,
he touches the line
gently

Fivehead

I've never minded
baldy jokes.
I greet people
with my forehead,
its great gleaming
expanse of oily skin
so large that one of
my friends calls it a
fivehead.
He says people can
see themselves in it.

I've thought
if people do notice
my shiny dome
they might not notice
my other flaws.

If they can see themselves
reflecting from my head
they can't see
through themselves
to me.

the drunk

caught
in a freeze-frame
vision,
bleared eyes fixed,
glass suspended,
salutes
the bottles
before him

Flesh remembers

She smelled of whiskey and blood—
not old blood, maybe half an hour
(it's still sticky at that stage
and comes off easily with peroxide
and a little rubbing)
—fresh enough that it could still remind me of
living things.

Her bones were broken
so I had to use both hands
and a lot of care
to place her arms over her chest
to get her ready for her mother,
but her skin was still pretty much intact which
helped,
because it remembered
—flesh remembers— ·
and so it held things like arm shape
for a little while longer,
but the base of her spine was cracked to one side
like a pencil that splintered in your fingers
but didn't quite separate
and her flesh memory wasn't strong enough
to hold the splinters in place,
so she lay in a grisly pelvic thrust
that I couldn't make myself rearrange,
not even for her mother.

The blood rubbed off her face easily
so she was pretty again
except for the smoky blue smudges under her eyes
that peroxide wouldn't take off because the blue was
blood under the skin.

I tried to clean the blood out of her hair
but only the scalp was holding her head together
—flesh remembers—
so I was rubbing skin over pulp
that should have been skull
but was—
at least I imagined it was
maybe it wasn't
but what if it was?
—brain instead
I felt like I was pushing my fingers
god oh god
into a water-ripe balloon
(but what if it burst?)
and then the mother was screaming
and screaming
and why did I ever take that fucking job
because my fingers . . .
my fingers remember

Between Ice and Shore

Minnesota

winter weaves
with the weight of ice
and glacial gray
walls of needles
day and day and day
warmth only
in the warp
of flesh
laced
dry
and stretched
on frozen loom.

middle age

white,
still slim,
shedding youth,
spotted and seamed
like a peeled birch

like a fly
cupped in the palm
of a hand too large
to know,
I wait

An institutional door
stands half open
beneath an exit sign
at the end of a silent hallway
of hard surfaces
reflecting
artificial light

ice
draws
light;
light
thaws
ice

icebreaker

ice is breaking;
where ice remains
shattered edges
are sharp with shards;
when the wind is right
the curious see
greater depths
in new water
between ice and shore

Lost
in an Old Timer
pocket knife,
folded,
lying at the back
of the drawer.

Judgment

swamps are drowning
and rain falls

islands of rooftops
form shingled headstones
and rain falls

days are dark,
heaven glowers,
and rain falls

spring rain
  river rain
summer rain
  lake rain
"fall, rain"

.

and rain falls

Communion

The arches
in the nave reach more directly
toward heaven
without leaden interference
from a roof.

The walls are worn
inside as out;
the air
is shared
with the sky.

The light,
filtered by
vaulted frames
to a holy
stone-rubbed
gold,
lures the eyes
up pitted stone
weathered
by communion.

Moment before

an ambiguous space:
waterwords
waiting for lock
to open,
waiting to flow
after dropping or
filling and lifting,
waiting for lock
to open,
to expose an upstream struggle
or a downstream slide,
waterwords
coming or going
to or from
an ambiguous space,
source too far back
to know,
arrival too far forward
to guess,
waterwords
waiting to flow
clear

file cabinet

cold, hard, smooth
locked
inside are men and women
date of birth, sex, parents with
textures of twenty pound bond
imprinted
by lives, addresses, marital
status in
neat rows of filed bodies
lying

Moment of Home

Standing,
foot crossed over foot,
shoulder pressed to bathroom wall—
head tipped to unforgiving wall—
wrists crossed over chest
in recollected grasp,
waiting
for a moment of home

About myself

I'll pull it out
before it's too late
because I love you
for your mind.
I love a good
tongue-lashing;
it makes me feel better
about myself.
You make me feel better
about myself.
Roll over.

lips wormaround words, writhing
in sinuousstruggle like eelsevading
the fishmonger's
pike

Nagasaki

teeth stand out
in those close enough
to the epicenter to be
charred
but not incinerated

teeth chatter
soundlessly
in smoke
and blackened flesh

bodies lie
in bones
of buildings

burned baby
suckles
burned breast
drinking death

he does and says love being one

i would be master of the small.
In my reactions with
and actions with
other people
i would be the embodiment
of the perfect tiny gesture;
the essence or aura
of a man
is the sum of the small things
he does and says.

Instead of
the missed gesture,
the overlooked birthday,
the forgotten appointment,
the tiny attempts to reach out that somehow feel
awkward
or faintly embarrassing,
as though I'm speaking of love
in a left-handed way
to a right-handed world,
i would say the word,
touch the shoulder,
accept the praise,
ease the way,
help, matter,
love.

Where my writing
contends with stuffy
and distant and large-oh-so-large,
it would be master of the sentence,
of the diction
that delights with tiny surprise
and small day to day knowing,
recognizing ourselves in others
and others in ourselves
so tiny bit by fractional bit,
perfect word by phrase by sentence,
the little writing comes
to the little devastation of
being.

Where all living seems huge,
i would be master of reducing it
to the tiniest number,
the number out of which all order,
all ordinals,
derive,
all words derive,
all gestures derive–
i would be the master of
one.

After Heavy Sailing

Facing the wind,
I see three tethered sailboats,
one with lone foresail unfurled,
in wind whipped water
as white as blue.

Facing the wind,
I know why
some weather-wise sailor
left that single torn sail

unfurled.
Something of defiance
should remain.

Two boats ride smoothly,
riding and rocking
but steady into the wind.

One plunges and lunges—
stem swinging,
swiveling, swinging,
as if searching for signs
of its lost wake—
under torn single sail

unfurled.
Something of defiance
should remain.

Facing the wind,
I envy two their tethers
but admire
the lone boat plunging.

Something of defiance
remains
unfurled.

Her face swells
like a bullfrog about to croak
and then she blows
word bile.
She has vomited rage for so long
she has only bile left.
It's green and sticks
to everyone
but me.
My teeth are showing
in a nonstick
smile that bile
slides off,
its dry heave aspirations
too slick
to stick.

I am a sailor who cannot
see the sea.
Northern Minnesota is over one thousand miles
from any ocean, so I am akin
to some Russians and Chinese and
all Tibetans, especially the monks, who
know dispossessed vastnesses of land
far from the salt source of all.
They pray
for their lives.

I cling to the Mississippi.

It does not give up the ocean,
but surrenders to it in
purposeful submission,
a lifeline thrown into the sea
one end gripped in stony fingers,
the other seasoned with salty promise for
monks and
landlocked sailors.

Mark Christensen teaches writing at Bemidji State University in Bemidji, Minnesota, where he was born. He earned his Ph.D. at the University of Minnesota after doing graduate work at the University of Wisconsin, Superior; the University of Minnesota, Duluth; and the Program in Writing at Breadloaf School of English, Vermont and Lincoln College, Oxford. He is also a photographer, fisherman, and swimmer.